Evaluating Arguments About
Animals

Simon Rose

CRABTREE
PUBLISHING COMPANY
WWW.CRABTREEBOOKS.COM

State Your Case

Author: Simon Rose

Series research and development: Reagan Miller

Editors: Sarah Eason, Claudia Martin, Jennifer Sanderson, and Janine Deschenes

Proofreader and indexer: Tracey Kelly

Editorial director: Kathy Middleton

Design: Paul Myerscough and Steve Mead

Cover design: Katherine Berti

Photo research: Claudia Martin

Production coordinator and Prepress technician:

Print coordinator: Katherine Berti

Produced for Crabtree Publishing Company
by Calcium Creative Ltd

Photo Credits:
t=Top, c=Center, b=Bottom, l=Left, r=Right.

Inside: Resolute: p.21; Shutterstock: Africa Studio: pp.3, 5; AG-Photos: p.32; Andrea Delbo: p.35; Andrey Burmakin: p.39; Anna50: p.43; AuntSpray: p.11; belizar: p.16; bh-2: pp.40–41; Bigandt.com: p.6; Christopher Halloran: p.26; Danae Abreu: p.42; David Tadevosian: p.4; Diane Garcia: p.25; Dionell Datiles: p.41; EcoPrint: p.7; GaudiLab: p.14; Hung Chung Chi: p.36; IPK Photography: p.20; Jack Dagley Photography: p.27; Jackson Stock Photography: p.24; Jnix: p.37; Jonathan Pledger: p.13; Kobby Dagan: p.22; Kosheleva Kristina: p.29; Lee Prince: p.17; Mendenhall Olga: p.19; Monkey Business Images: pp.10, 31; Pixinoo: p.9; Richard Seeley: p.18; Shishkin Dmitry: p.38; sirtravelalot: p.30; Steve Ikeguchi: p.12; Steve Oehlenschlager: p.23; Unchalee Khun: p.28; Vgstockstudio: p.8; Volodymyr Burdiak: pp.1, 15; wavebreakmedia: p.34; Yuttana Jaowattana: p.33.

Cover: All images from Shutterstock

Library and Archives Canada Cataloguing in Publication

Rose, Simon, 1961-, author
    Evaluating arguments about animals / Simon Rose.

(State your case)
Includes bibliographical references and index.
Issued in print and electronic formats.
ISBN 978-0-7787-5075-8 (hardcover).--
ISBN 978-0-7787-5088-8 (softcover).--
ISBN 978-1-4271-2160-8 (HTML)

    1. Animal welfare--Juvenile literature. 2. Animal welfare--Moral andethical aspects--Juvenile literature. 3. Animal rights--Juvenile literature. 4. Critical thinking--Juvenile literature. 5. Thought and thinking—Juvenileliterature. 6. Reasoning--Juvenile literature. 7. Persuasion (Rhetoric)--Juvenile literature. I. Title.

HV4708.R664 2018   j636.08'32   C2018-903025-9
                                              C2018-903026-7

Library of Congress Cataloging-in-Publication Data

Names: Rose, Simon, 1961- author.
Title: Evaluating arguments about animals / Simon Rose.
Description: New York, New York : Crabtree Publishing Company, [2019] | Series: State your case |
  Includes bibliographical references and index.
Identifiers: LCCN 2018030277 (print) | LCCN 2018032293 (ebook) |
  ISBN 9781427121608 (Electronic) |
  ISBN 9780778750758 (hardcover) |
  ISBN 9780778750888 (paperback)
Subjects: LCSH: Animal rights. | Animal welfare.
Classification: LCC HV4708 (ebook) |
  LCC HV4708 .R67 2019 (print) | DDC 179/.3--dc23
LC record available at https://lccn.loc.gov/2018030277

Crabtree Publishing Company
www.crabtreebooks.com   1-800-387-7650

Printed in the U.S.A./092018/CG20180810

Published in Canada
Crabtree Publishing
616 Welland Ave.
St. Catharines, Ontario
L2M 5V6

Published in the United States
Crabtree Publishing
PMB 59051
350 Fifth Avenue, 59th Floor
New York, New York 10118

Published in the United Kingdom
Crabtree Publishing
Maritime House
Basin Road North, Hove
BN41 1WR

Published in Australia
Crabtree Publishing
3 Charles Street
Coburg North
VIC, 3058

CONTENTS

CHAPTER 1

ANIMALS TODAY AND TOMORROW

Animals and **animal welfare** are always topics of strong discussion. Many people feel very strongly about animal issues because they love animals and believe humans have a responsibility to protect them. There are many national and international organizations concerned with animal welfare.

Animals and People

Vegetarians do not eat meat or fish, while **vegans** do not use or eat any animal products, such as leather, milk, and honey. However, animals such as cows, chickens, pigs, sheep, and some fish are kept for eating by humans. Some food animals are kept in large facilities known as **factory farms**. Many meat-eaters are concerned by the conditions in these facilities and take care to buy meat only from animals that have roamed freely in fields and spacious enclosures.

Animals and people have worked together for thousands of years. Sometimes they have worked at carrying loads or pulling machinery on farms and for other **industries**. In some parts of the world, this is still the case, with donkeys at work on Egyptian farms, yaks in Nepal, and water buffalo pulling plows in India. In many places, **service animals** such as guide dogs work closely with people with disabilities, helping to improve their lives. Many people also enjoy keeping pets, from goldfish and tortoises to dogs and mice.

Many farm animals that are used for food live in cramped conditions. Some people believe that the animals should be treated more humanely.

Service animals are not pets. They are trained to work with people who need help.

For generations, some animals have been removed from their natural **habitats** and placed in **safari parks** and zoos. Animals are also used in sports and entertainment. They perform in **rodeo sports** and as stunt animals in movies and television shows. In some parts of the world, people watch **bullfighting** or performing bears. Millions of animals are also still used in scientific testing for products such as medications and **cosmetics**. There are many critics of all these practices, with some people **campaigning** against them.

Controlling Animal Populations

Animal populations in the wild sometimes need to be reduced. This may be to reduce the number of a certain **species** that is damaging an **ecosystem**, or to control diseases that are spread by certain animals. The process of reducing wild animal numbers is called **culling**. Some people do not agree with culling and believe that humans beings should not disturb nature.

Sometimes animal populations have been so strictly controlled that an entire area has been cleared of a certain species. This happened with wolves in many parts of the world because farmers killed them to protect farm animals. However, in recent years, wolves have been reintroduced in certain areas, although some people worry that this is dangerous for cattle and humans as wolves are fierce **predators**.

Is Extinction Forever?

Thousands of species of animals, including elephants, rhinoceroses, and tigers, are in danger of **extinction** through **poaching** or habitat destruction. Other animals have already been driven to extinction.

Today, some scientists are considering **cloning tissue** samples of extinct animals to bring them back. Though this could be a good thing, some people believe that it is a step too far for humans.

Animals: A Hot Topic

There are many debates and conflicting opinions about animals and animal welfare. For example, many people wonder if factory farms should be banned and argue that animals should not be used in scientific and medical tests. Others think that humans should not keep animals as pets, and that animals should not be used for any kind of work or entertainment. Others still argue that animals should be used for varying kinds of labor, as they have been throughout history.

Arguing About Animals

You probably often hear, read, and see friends, family, scientists, and newscasters offering strong opinions about animals and their relationship with humans. You need to be able to evaluate the arguments to decide which ones are **credible**— and which are not. That way, you can start to form your own opinions about animal issues and your own relationship with animals.

In this book, we'll take a look at arguments about animal issues. We'll examine the features of an argument, what makes a strong argument, and how to decide if you agree with it or not. Let's start by taking a look at the argument about animal culling on the opposite page.

Some animals do work for humans. Sheepdogs herd, or control, flocks of sheep. Sniffer dogs help police officers find illegal drugs or explosives. Other dogs are trained to find people who are lost in the wild or after a natural disaster.

Do You Agree?

"Should animal culling be allowed?"

CULLING OF ANIMALS SHOULD BE ALLOWED.

Sometimes one species of animal is culled to protect another. For example, in the United Kingdom (UK), badgers are culled because they spread a disease called bovine tuberculosis, which is very dangerous for cattle. Cormorants, a type of bird, threaten fish in the Columbia River Basin in Oregon. Blaine Parker of the Columbia Inter-Tribal Fish Commission says that, although it seems strange to kill one species to protect another, sometimes it is necessary to do so.

Animals also need to be culled to protect people's livelihoods. Some animals, such as deer, damage crops, and seals can destroy fishermen's nets. In the United States, more than 4 million animals were killed in 2013 because they were a threat to farms, property, **natural resources**, or health and safety. Sometimes animals are killed when they endanger people. In Australia, saltwater crocodiles killed 33 people between 1971 and 2016, so they are sometimes culled.

CULLING OF ANIMALS SHOULD NOT BE ALLOWED.

There are other methods of controlling animal populations to prevent them from damaging other species, the environment, or people. Animals can be **relocated**, or moved, from places where they are a threat to other species. For example, noise devices can scare seals away from fishing nets.

Humans should not interfere with nature. When they do, it causes imbalance in the ecosystem. In some cases, animal **overpopulation** is the fault of humans in the first place. When humans hunt predators, it results in higher populations of **prey**. For example, hunting wolves means that the deer population grows, because there are fewer wolves to eat them. Then, deer may damage farmers' fields. The problem began with humans hunting.

Culling might lead to the extinction of some species. In Australia, more than 1.5 million kangaroos were culled in 2015 to protect grasslands from **overgrazing**. Brad Smith of Upper Hunter Valley Wildlife Aid believes that kangaroos are threatened by culling: "If you take into account the numbers of kangaroos shot each year and the numbers hit and killed by cars, it's running into millions."

After reading the arguments about whether culling should be allowed, decide which side you agree with. How did you make your choice? Did you rely on personal experience? Does the way the arguments are presented influence your decision?

Instead of culling dangerous saltwater crocodiles, in recent years, they have been relocated.

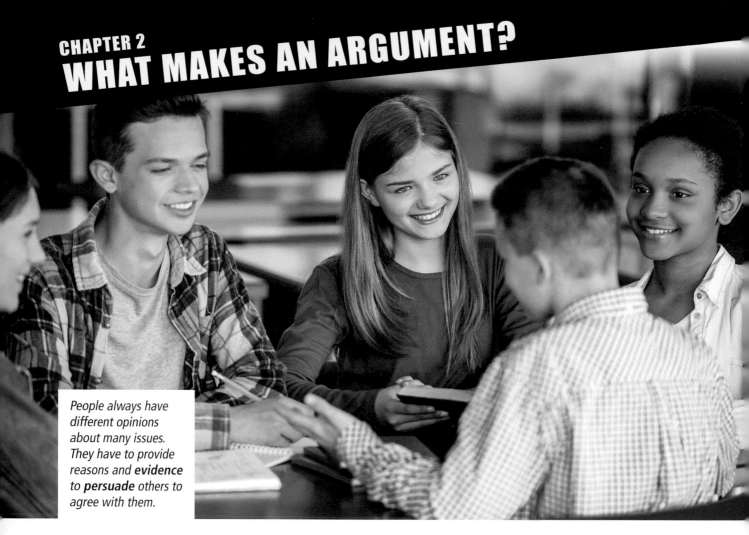

*People always have different opinions about many issues. They have to provide reasons and **evidence** to **persuade** others to agree with them.*

An argument is a set of reasons based on **logic**. It shows that a person's belief or position on an issue is **valid**, or correct. An argument can be used to try to change another person's point of view, or to persuade them to accept a new point of view. Arguments can also be used to draw support or promote action for a cause.

Why Argue?

You read, hear, and see arguments every day. For example, you might see two dog-lovers arguing about which type of dog makes the best pet. You might see people discussing whether a local zoo should be shut down. One person might think the zoo is a great local activity, and the other might say it is cruel to keep animals in **captivity**. In an argument, a person states their ideas, gives their reasons, and, if the argument is strong, supports

their reasons with evidence to try to persuade the other person that their ideas are best.

Arguments can be used in different ways. Sometimes an argument can help people learn about an issue. It might explain one or both sides of an issue, so that people can make an informed decision about what they believe. For example, it might explain why some people choose to become vegetarians or vegans.

Other arguments are used to gather support for a cause, such as trying to persuade people not to eat fish species that are being threatened by **overfishing**. This type of argument is meant to influence the way you think about something, or to change your mind about an issue.

Other arguments are used to solve problems and make decisions. For example, members of a local community might present arguments for creating new community rules that protect a local plant species from being picked. When both sides of an argument are heard, people can come to a decision about how they should act on an issue.

Arguments are not always serious. Sometimes people present arguments to learn about and discuss opposing ideas.

Prove Your Point

Arguments are made up of a set of **claims**, or statements, that prove why a position is right. To prove that your argument is correct, you also need to give evidence that supports your claims. Without evidence, there is no way to prove that your claims are true. When you are evaluating an argument, it is up to you to decide whether the person making the argument has supported their claims with evidence.

Overfishing is one of the biggest threats to the health of the world's oceans and the animals that live there. Each day, tons of fish are hauled out of the water. This is much more than can be naturally replenished, lowering fish populations.

Building an Argument

A strong argument has the following features, or parts:

Core Argument

The **core argument** is your position, or where you stand, on the topic or issue. It is the main point that you will try to prove in your argument. Arguments state the core argument in their introduction. An example of a core argument is:

> *The tissue of extinct animals should not be cloned.*

Claims

Your claims are the statements that support your core argument. An example of a claim is:

> *Cloning animals will create issues for natural ecosystems.*

Reasons

Reasons are details that support your claim. Reasons explain why you have made that specific claim. An example of a reason is:

> *Since they have died out and the ecosystem has **adapted** without them, bringing back extinct animals might threaten other animals in an ecosystem and damage the environment. Some animals become extinct for natural reasons, such as being unable to adapt to a changing climate. If these animals were brought back to life, they would struggle to survive.*

> *There are always different sides to an argument. Each side usually has a number of reasons for their beliefs and evidence to support them.*

Evidence

A good argument supports its reasons with evidence. Evidence might be a quotation from an interview with someone who is considered to be an expert on the topic. It could be facts about the topic, or **statistics** from a study of people affected by an issue. Without evidence, an argument cannot be proven to be true.

> Not all of the evidence you find is credible, so you need to assess if it is valid. You can do this by asking questions, such as:
> - Who is the author of the source of information? Are they qualified to speak on the subject?
> - Did the information come from a respected organization, such as a government website?
> - Is the source up to date? A source that is several years old may have outdated information.
> - Can you find similar information on other respected sites? If not, you may need to evaluate whether the source is credible.

This is an example of credible evidence. It comes from a respected organization and someone who is knowledgeable about the subject:

> *In many parts of the world, **invasive species** of animals and plants cause damage to the ecosystem. The same thing could happen if cloned species were reintroduced after being extinct. Beth Shapiro, evolutionary biologist at University of California, Santa Cruz, has concerns about bringing back the extinct passenger pigeon. "I worry about the dramatic changes to the forest in the eastern part of the North American continent," she says. She explains further that before any decision can be made about bringing back the bird, we need to understand more about it and the impact it could have on the habitat.*

Counterclaims

To make an argument even stronger, a person needs to take note of the possible **counterclaims** against his or her argument. Counterclaims are the opposing claims, or the claims that support the opposite viewpoint to the argument. After making claims and giving reasons and evidence, a person making an argument should write down the strongest counterclaim against their argument. They should then respond to the counterclaim, using evidence, to prove why their argument is stronger. This is an example of a counterclaim:

> *While some animals became extinct naturally, other species died out because of humans hunting them or destroying their habitat. For example, the dodo became extinct soon after humans arrived in its island home, Mauritius, in the seventeenth century. Many people believe we should correct the wrongs of the past by cloning the dodo. However, as biologist Beth Shapiro explains, bringing back extinct animals into ecosystems that function without them could have negative effects.*

Conclusion

Your conclusion should restate your main argument and reasons. An example of a conclusion is:

> *If extinct animals were reintroduced, they might struggle to survive, threaten other animals, or damage the environment. Given these issues, it is clear that extinct animals should not be cloned.*

The dodo was a large, flightless bird that lived on the island of Mauritius in the Indian Ocean.

Evaluating an Argument

You can evaluate an argument by looking at its features. Examine the argument below about hunting. Does the argument include all of the features it needs to be a strong argument? When you have finished reading, decide if you think this argument is strong.

CORE ARGUMENT

Hunting animals for sport is wrong.

CLAIM

Hunting for sport causes unnecessary suffering to animals.

REASON

Hunting causes animals to suffer if they are not killed with one shot. If the hunter misses their target and the animal escapes, the animal's injuries could mean that it suffers in great pain.

EVIDENCE

In the United States, hunters kill more than 200 million animals every year. In many cases, the animals do not die instantly. Some may eventually die from their wounds, while others may die from starvation if their wound is severe enough to prevent them from searching for food. A member of the Maine BowHunters Alliance estimates that 50 percent of animals shot with crossbows are wounded but not killed. According to People for the **Ethical** Treatment of Animals (PETA), 11 percent of deer shot by hunters die only after being shot two or more times, while some wounded deer suffer for more than 15 minutes before dying.

*Hunting is part of a way of life for many people, and it is also an important contributor to the local **economy**.*

CLAIM

Hunting could cause some species of animals to become extinct.

REASON

If too many adults of a species are killed, there will not be enough animals of breeding age to have offspring. If not enough babies are born, the animal population will start to decline. Sometimes very young animals are killed, so these animals cannot reproduce at all.

EVIDENCE

Hunting has caused animal extinctions in the past. The Tasmanian tiger, the **great auk,** the **quagga, Steller's sea cow**, and the dodo were all hunted to extinction. According to the Worldwide Fund for Nature, elephants, rhinoceroses, and tigers are currently in danger of extinction due to hunting and poaching.

COUNTERCLAIM

People who are in favor of hunting maintain that, in many African countries, governments cannot spare the money to pay for protecting animals such as lions, rhinos, and elephants. The money from hunting tourism helps protect the other animals and also provides local people with jobs. However, money from **trophy hunting** only benefits those who organize the hunting. This is a small group in the local community. For example, around 9,000 hunters visit South Africa every year. According to the South African government, this generates revenue of around $462 million. However, the UN Food and Agricultural Organization found that only 3 percent of hunting revenue reached local people. "Local communities are key stakeholders for **conservation** initiatives," says Roderick Campbell of Economists at Large, "yet they receive minimal benefits from trophy hunting."

CONCLUSION

It is clear that hunting causes unnecessary suffering for animals and can also lead to the extinction of certain species. For these reasons, it is clear that hunting animals for sport is wrong.

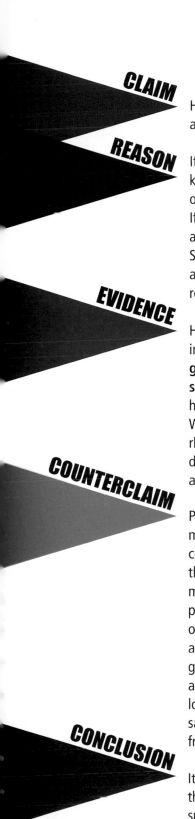

White rhinos are killed for their horns, which are used in herbal medicines in some cultures.

Making a Great Argument

One way to make a strong argument is to target it at your audience. You can base your argument on details about your audience, such as their age, **gender**, or background.

Animal and animal welfare issues are very personal, and many people have their own strong opinions. An audience made up of people who are interested in a topic must be approached differently from those who are not familiar with it. For example, a dog owner may have stronger opinions about the location of a dog park than someone with no pets. People of different ages have different perspectives on issues. Other details, such as a person's lifestyle, their job, and where they live, may also affect how they feel about issues. For example, someone who lives in a city and has never been hunting may have a perspective on the sport that is different from someone who lives on a farm. When you make an argument, it is important to keep your audience in mind, and ensure that your claims and evidence will relate to them.

Introductions Count

Your introduction should get the reader or listener interested in the topic. Before stating your core argument, include a statement that interests the reader.

For example, the introduction to an argument against hunting could state:

> *Did you know that, in 2012, trophy hunters killed 617 lions in South Africa just for sport? Lions are considered **vulnerable** to extinction, which means that if hunting and habitat loss continue at their current rate, one day there will be no more lions. This is why I believe that hunting is wrong.*

Group discussions are useful for gathering different opinions about an issue. Some people may have formed their judgments from personal experience, while others may have ethical reasons for their opinions. Listening to different viewpoints may help you form counterclaims to your own argument.

One way to help an audience relate to an argument about hunting is to describe the impact hunting has on animals they are familiar with.

Clincher Conclusions

The conclusion is as important as your introduction. It restates your core argument and claims. Your conclusion should end with a **clincher**. This is a statement that strengthens your argument by capturing the audience's attention right at the end.

In the argument against hunting, your clincher could state:

> Given the evidence, hunting not only causes damage to the species that is hunted but also to other animals and the environment. If predators such as wolves are wiped out by hunting, animals that they eat, such as deer, will increase in numbers. This, in turn, could lead to too many plants being eaten by the deer, taking food from other animals. The ecosystem is balanced to benefit all wild animals. Hunting destroys that balance. So, for that reason alone, it should be banned.

A clincher can also be a quote or a question that makes the reader think, such as:

> Shouldn't we be trying to protect animals rather than killing them for fun? Do we really want to live in a world where lions, tigers, elephants, rhinos, and so many other animals no longer exist?

Choose Your Words

The words you use and how you use them will help persuade people to see and appreciate your point of view. Words can appeal to someone's emotions and strengthen the evidence that you present. For example, referring to sources of facts and statistics will back up your claims. Mentioning qualified experts and quoting from them will also make people more likely to believe you. Words can appeal to people's emotions by emphasizing things they care about. In the hunting argument, words might emphasize the suffering of animals compared to benefits of protecting wildlife, now and for future generations.

Powerful Words

How effective an argument is often depends on the types of words used. **Rhetoric** is the art of using language effectively when writing or speaking. Rhetoric is usually used in persuasive speaking or writing by appealing to a reader's or listener's emotions.

Persuasive Trio

There are three types of rhetoric: logos, pathos, and ethos.

Logos: Logos is an ancient Greek word from which we get the word "logic." Facts and statistics are often used in logical arguments. Backing up claims with solid facts will help others consider your position, even if they do not agree with it. Here is an example of logos:

> *Vampire bats spread a disease called **rabies**, causing the deaths of thousands of livestock and even some humans in Latin America. Culling vampire bats since 1980 has led to around a 90 percent reduction in cases of rabies in dogs and people. However, the deaths of livestock still means that local farmers lose around $30 million every year.*

Pathos: An argument based on pathos appeals to the audience's emotions with personal stories. Stating that people have caught rabies from vampire bats may not relate to audience members who have never seen a case of rabies or are not familiar with the disease. However, a story about a person dealing with rabies not only appeals to the audience's emotions but also provides an example to show why the statistic is important. Pathos should be used only to support your claim. It should not be used to confuse or frighten people in order to win an argument. A good example of pathos is:

> *In 2004, 15-year-old Jeanna was bitten by a vampire bat on her finger. Her mother dressed the wound, and at first, everything seemed fine. Three weeks later, Jeanna's finger began to feel numb and tingly. She then felt tired, nauseous, and developed double vision. Her family took her to the hospital, where her condition rapidly worsened. Tests found that Jeanna had rabies. Her parents were told she had only hours to live. Fortunately, an infectious disease specialist was able to help Jeanna. She spent 11 weeks in the hospital and is lucky to have made a full recovery.*

Blood is the main food source for most types of vampire bats. The species can be found in Mexico and other Central and South American countries.

Ethos: Ethos is language that shows that the speaker can be trusted. The person can tell the audience about their experience with the topic. Using reliable sources to build your argument can also create ethos. A speaker can also establish trust with the audience by respecting the opposing view and presenting it fairly. An example of ethos would be:

> *As a dog trainer with 25 years' experience, I have reviewed hundreds of dog-training programs over the years. I believe that this program is one of the best programs that I have ever seen. Owners are encouraged never to shout at or punish their pets. Instead, owners are taught the benefits of establishing trust, discipline, and affection.*

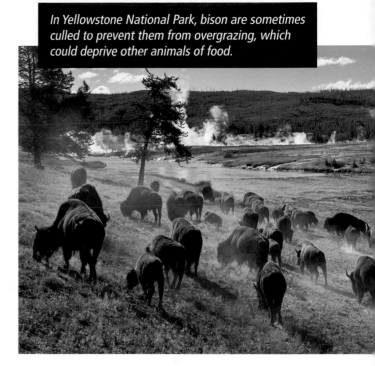

In Yellowstone National Park, bison are sometimes culled to prevent them from overgrazing, which could deprive other animals of food.

LOOKING AT LANGUAGE

Read the following statement. Can you identify the rhetoric the author has used?

Culling animals can protect ecosystems and eliminate disease. In Yellowstone National Park, it was decided in the winter of 2017 to 2018 to reduce the bison population to 900 animals from around 1,400. The bison were culled to prevent them from overgrazing, leading to possible starvation for other animals. Bison also carry the disease brucellosis, which causes serious health issues in cattle. This affects not only local cows but the farmers who rely on them for their livelihood. How much more damage do you think would be done to the Yellowstone ecosystem and the livelihoods of local farmers if bison were not culled?

Which types of rhetoric does the statement use to appeal to the audience? What words or phrases make you think so?

Where Do You Stand?

Read these two arguments about whether the U.S. government should reintroduce wolves into Rocky Mountain National Park, in Colorado, where they were wiped out by hunting. Keep in mind the features of an argument and the power of language. Which argument do you feel is stronger? Why?

Wolves Should Be Reintroduced in Rocky Mountain National Park.

Wolves are supposed to be part of the Rocky Mountain ecosystem and are needed to control the numbers of other species. Since wolves were wiped out of the region by hunting in the early twentieth century, the elk population has grown out of control, overgrazing the park's meadows and depriving other species of food. In 1995, eight wolves were reintroduced to Yellowstone National Park in Idaho, Montana, and Wyoming. At the time, elk and deer populations had grown very large and were damaging trees and shrubs where birds live. Since 1995, elk and deer populations have fallen, and birds have returned.

Farmers worry that wolves kill their livestock, but there are ways to prevent this, including fences and **GPS** devices to follow wolf movements. In any case, coyotes and big cats kill more farm animals than wolves do. In 2010, according to the U.S. Department of Agriculture (USDA), coyotes were responsible for 53.1 percent of livestock deaths.

Wolves are also not dangerous to people. There have been no attacks on humans since wolves returned to Yellowstone. In North America, there were 20 to 30 wolf attacks on people, only 3 of them causing death, between 1900 and 2000. In the same period, brown bears killed 71 people in North America.

The presence of wolves can draw tourists to an area. According to a survey by Yellowstone National Park, an average of 14,285 people per year visited Yellowstone to view wolves between 1995 and 2002. This brings money into the local economy and helps to maintain the park.

Based on the fact that wolves are a vital part of the ecosystem, are not dangerous to people, attack far fewer livestock than other animals, and encourage tourism, wolves should be reintroduced to Rocky Mountain National Park.

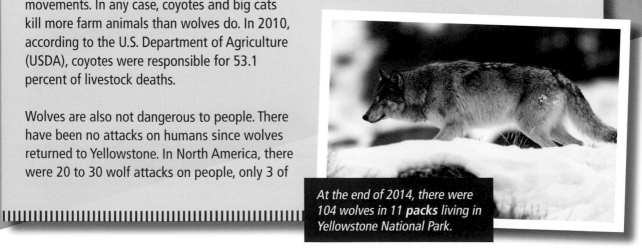

At the end of 2014, there were 104 wolves in 11 **packs** living in Yellowstone National Park.

Wolves Should Not Be Reintroduced in Rocky Mountain National Park.

The return of wolves to Rocky Mountain National Park would threaten livestock such as sheep and cows, along with the livelihoods of farmers. According to the USDA, wolves killed 8,100 cattle in 2010. The loss of revenue to farmers and ranchers was $3,646,000. Hunters also have their livelihoods threatened since they are competing with wolves when they hunt deer and elk.

It was the U.S. government that decided to reintroduce wolves into national parks, such as Yellowstone, in the western United States. It is estimated that reintroducing one wolf into the wild costs between $200,000 and $1 million. This money could be better spent on other programs, such as protecting the environment or other species.

Although wolves may help to increase tourism and help the local economy, this is not always a good thing. Tourism means more traffic, building more roads and hotels, more garbage generated by tourists, and more people damaging the environment. More encounters between humans and wild animals are also likely with the increase of tourism. These encounters often end in injury for both people and animals.

Wolves should not be reintroduced to Rocky Mountain National Park because of the harm they cause to livestock and the livelihoods of farmers and hunters. Reintroduction programs are also very expensive, and the money could be better spent on other wildlife programs.

Tourism can cause problems in national parks. People often get dangerously close to wild animals to try to take photographs of them.

CHAPTER 3

SHOULD ANIMALS BE USED IN RODEO SPORTS?

Rodeo sports involve the use of horses, cattle, and other farm animals. Rodeo events are based on the skills of men and women who work with these animals. Events include **steer** wrestling, wagon racing, bull and **bronc riding**, calf roping, and barrel racing. Although rodeos are exciting to watch and take part in, many people worry about the welfare of rodeo animals.

Community and Tradition

Rodeo developed from the daily working routines of people herding cattle in North and South America, Australia, and New Zealand. Today, rodeo is a professional sport and is popular in the western United States, western Canada, and northern Mexico. Rodeo is closely associated with local communities and traditions. Its supporters see rodeo as part of their heritage and history, especially in **rural** communities. Many of them work with animals on a daily basis and see nothing wrong with having sporting events in which professionals can showcase their skills.

Professional associations run rodeo sports, set the rules, and look after the welfare of the animals, making sure that they receive veterinary care. Many spectators attend rodeos, which brings in a lot of money. For example, the Calgary Stampede in Alberta, which features many rodeo events, is a major tourist attraction in Canada.

Entertainment or Cruelty?

Many people are opposed to rodeo sports. They believe that rodeo sports harm animals, claiming that in many events, animals are terrified and that many animals are injured and killed each year because of rodeo sports. They argue that animals should never suffer for the entertainment of people.

Rodeos are incredibly popular. In 2017, 1.2 million people visited the Calgary Stampede.

Rodeo sports are not popular with everyone. Animal welfare groups regularly protest against events that they believe are cruel to the animals involved.

Animal welfare groups across North America campaign against rodeo sports and argue that they should be banned.

Events that are of particular concern include calf roping. In calf roping, the young animal is pulled by a rope around its neck that is held by a person on a horse. The calf is pulled into the air and thrown to the ground, then its legs are tied together. Calves sometimes suffer neck injuries or are even killed. However, fans of this event point out that a calf is a strong animal that weighs between 225 and 250 pounds (102 and 113 kg). Rodeo professionals handle the animals with great skill. After the brief event, calves usually get up and trot away without signs of distress. In steer wrestling, the animal's head is twisted until it falls to the ground, which can also result in neck injury. In **chuck wagon** racing at the Calgary Stampede, teams of horses pull wagons around a course at speeds that animal welfare campaigners say creates unnecessary risk.

Some other countries, such as the Netherlands and the UK, do not allow rodeos. Other countries restrict some events to protect the animals. For example, Germany does not allow calf roping.

So what are the arguments for and against animals being used in rodeo sports?

RODEO BY NUMBERS

Here are some interesting statistics about rodeos:

- Up to 30 million people attend around 550 Professional Rodeo Cowboys Association (PRCA) rodeos across the United States each year.
- Around 50 Canadian Professional Rodeo Association (CPRA) events take place across Canada every year.
- The Reno Rodeo in Nevada is estimated to generate around $42 million for the local economy.

Animals Should Be Used in Rodeo Sports.

Animals used in rodeo sports are well cared for, so there is no reason to stop using them. Rodeo organizers and professionals care about animal welfare. It would make no sense for them to mistreat animals that need to be in top condition for rodeo events. Riders treat the animals like top athletes that need to be looked after. Rodeo animal owners also spend a lot of money to keep their animals healthy, so that they can compete. Rodeo associations across the United States and Canada set the rules of rodeo and for animal safety. The PRCA, which was set up in 1947, has 60 rules about how animals are cared for and handled. There are regulations that state **spurs** cannot be sharp, that an animal's head should be wrapped for protection, and that animals must be removed from events if they are injured. There are also rules about a veterinarian being onsite at rodeo events. People who break the rules about animal safety are fined or kicked out of competitions. Rodeo animals are often only in rodeo events briefly each time. Most bucking horses or bulls work fewer than 5 minutes at a rodeo per year. Between rodeos, they are kept in good conditions and have good food and veterinary care. In Canada, the Calgary Stampede has a farm for retired rodeo animals, where they live happily in open fields.

Rodeo animals are not mistreated to make them perform. Horses and bulls buck naturally. They are not forced to do so. Bucking does not cause the animal any pain. Rodeo rules state that animals cannot be hurt to make them buck. John Barnes, livestock superintendent for the Wrangler National Finals Rodeo in Las Vegas, explains,

Rodeo professionals say that bulls are not forced to buck. They buck naturally when a rodeo rider climbs on their back.

"I've been raised around livestock, and they only perform as well as they feel. They have to be at their peak health to perform at their peak ability. The cattle break from the box faster when they feel good. It's the same with the horses and the bulls." Rodeo riders also cannot use an electric **prod** or otherwise hurt animals while they are in the **chute** to make them angry. The electric cattle prod was developed by a veterinarian and simply gives the animal a very small shock that does not hurt. The prod is used only on the shoulder of an animal that will not leave the chute to enter the rodeo arena. "It can be very dangerous [for riders] in the chute," says Cindy Schonholtz of the PRCA. "Our goal is to get that animal safely out."

People who oppose rodeos say that, even though rodeo associations have rules to keep animals safe, rodeo events can still cause injury or death. While it is true that animals have been injured or died in rodeo events, the rates are very low, less than 1 percent. Most rodeo animals live long lives and can perform well for many years. Bulls can still be in rodeos at the age of 15 and horses at age 25.

Based on the fact that animals are treated well, are not abused, receive veterinary care, and are protected by the rules of rodeo, animals should be used in rodeo sports. Professional rodeo associations have strict regulations about animal welfare and ensure the safety of the animal competitors because, without them, the sport would not exist.

Rodeo bulls are very powerful animals. Some can weigh around 1,500 pounds (680 kg). Very few riders stay on the bull for long at rodeo events.

Animals Should Not Be Used in Rodeo Sports.

Rodeo events are dangerous and can cause injury or death to animals. Rodeo animals are not like human athletes. Humans have a choice whether to take part in their sport. Animals do not. In 2001, a calf had to be **euthanized** after suffering a broken hind leg at the Calgary Stampede roping event. At the Cloverdale Rodeo in British Columbia in 2004, a cow's neck was broken during steer racing, and the animal had to be killed. A steer also suffered a broken neck during steer wrestling at the Calgary Stampede in 2013. The same year, at the Cheyenne Frontier Days in Wyoming, an animal was badly hurt in the calf roping event. A steer's leg was also broken during the steer wrestling, and the animal had to be killed. More than 60 horses have been killed in chuck wagon racing at the Calgary Stampede since 1986. These deaths are caused by injuries in crashes or when horses are so stressed that they have a heart attack. The American Society for the Prevention of Cruelty to Animals (ASPCA) says that rodeos are "a cruel form of entertainment that involves the painful, stressful, and potentially harmful treatment of livestock." Dr. Robert Fetzner, Director of Slaughter Operations for the USDA Food Safety and Inspection Service, states that he has seen injuries to cattle that have been used in rodeos and later sent for slaughter, or killing. Injuries he has noted include broken ribs and legs, and broken necks caused by roping.

Calf roping is considered to be animal cruelty by those opposed to rodeos, even if this event is part of North American culture and tradition.

Young animals used in steer wrestling can suffer terrible injuries so that human winners can collect large amounts in prize money.

Animals are sometimes mistreated so that they will perform well in the rodeo arena. The noisy crowd and strange atmosphere in the arena means that some animals may be frightened. Despite what rodeo supporters say, bucking is not natural behavior. Horses and bulls buck because a strap is tied tightly around their middle, and they are trying to get it off. The spurs on the riders' boots are also used to make horses and bulls buck and kick. The PRCA allows animals to be shocked with prods if they are too slow running out of the chute. The use of bucking straps, electric prods, and other devices are "taking animals that are normally tame, **docile** animals and then provoking them … to be fierce and aggressive," says Lindsay Rajt of People for the Ethical Treatment of Animals (PETA).

It is true that the PRCA has strict rules about the conduct of rodeos and the treatment of animals. However, it could be argued that rodeo organizers care only about rodeo animals because they are worth a lot of money and can win huge cash prizes for the riders, as well as bring in money from tickets sold for rodeo events. "All the rules that are in the rodeo really exist to protect the rider and not the animal," says Lindsay Rajt of PETA.

Based on the evidence that animals sometimes suffer severe stress, injuries, and death in rodeo events, animals should not be used in rodeo sports. Although the sport does have rules and remains very popular, it is clear that rodeo is in the best interests of the organizers, competitors, and audiences, but not of the animals.

25

STATE YOUR CASE

When it comes to any issue, you have to look at arguments on both sides before you decide where you stand. Remember the features of effective arguments when you think about arguments for and against animals being used in rodeo sports. Which side's argument do you think is stronger? Why do you think so? Use the "In Summary: For and Against" list to help you figure out your decision, and state your own case.

IN SUMMARY: FOR AND AGAINST

For Animals Being Used in Rodeo Sports

Rodeo organizers and professionals care about animal welfare.

- Riders treat the animals like top athletes that need to be looked after.
- Rodeo associations set many rules about animal safety and care.
- People who break the rules are fined or kicked out from competitions.
- Rodeo animals are often only in rodeo events briefly each time.
- The Calgary Stampede has a farm for retired rodeo animals.

Rodeo animals are not mistreated to make them perform.

- Horses and bulls do not need to be forced to buck. They do it naturally.
- Rodeo rules state that nothing that hurts the animal can be used on or under a strap to make them buck.
- Riders do not prod or hurt animals in the chute to make them angry. They only do so to ensure the safety of the animal and rider.
- Spurs used by cowboys are not sharp.

Modern rodeo events are based on traditional cattle ranching practices, such as roping cattle for sale, in the western United States, western Canada, and northern Mexico.

Against Animals Being Used in Rodeo Sports

Rodeo events are dangerous and can cause injury or death to animals.

- Animals sometimes suffer terrible injuries at rodeos. In calf roping, the young animal can suffer neck injuries or be killed. In steer wrestling, the animal's neck can be broken.
- More than 60 horses have been killed in chuck wagon racing at the Calgary Stampede since 1986.

Some rodeo events, such as chuck wagon racing, are very dangerous for both people and animals. Horses have to be euthanized after suffering injuries such as broken legs in racing.

Animals are sometimes mistreated so that they will perform well in the rodeo arena.

- The noisy crowd and strange atmosphere in the arena means that some animals may be frightened.
- Horses and bulls buck because a strap is tied tightly around their middle, and because of the spurs on the rider.
- The PRCA allows animals to be shocked with prods if they are too slow running out of the chute.
- According to PETA, the use of bucking straps, electric prods, and other devices encourages animals "to be fierce and aggressive."

CHAPTER 4

SHOULD ANIMALS BE KEPT AS PETS?

In 2016, Americans owned more than 200 million pets, including 70 million dogs and 74 million cats, plus birds, fish, rabbits, ferrets, rodents, and reptiles. In Canada, 7.5 million households own pets, with 5.9 million dogs and 7.9 million cats. However, some people feel that animals do not belong in our homes. Are there downsides to keeping animals as pets?

The Benefits of Pets

People who are in favor of pets argue that keeping pets is good for both the animal and the owner. The animal has a home, food, and—in most cases—has longer **life expectancy** than animals living in the wild. Humans have **bred** animals, including dogs, cats, rabbits, and guinea pigs, as pets over hundreds or even thousands of years. The dog was the first animal to be **domesticated**, or tamed, by humans, at least 14,000 years ago. Domesticated animals could not survive on their own in the wild.

People also benefit from having animals around them. Pets can improve the **mental health** of their owners by giving them companionship and helping them release stress. Pets can also teach children about responsibility if they help with feeding, cleaning, and exercising. A 2017 study in Sweden found that, for people living alone, having a dog as a pet lowered their risk of death from heart problems by 36 percent. This is believed to be partly due to the exercise that they get while walking or playing with dogs, but may also be the result of lower stress levels.

People usually become very attached to their pets. Most pet owners consider the animals in their homes to be part of their family.

We provide pet animals with many comforts, such as living spaces and toys. But shouldn't they be in their natural environment?

Should Animals Be Free?

Some people believe that animals do not belong in our homes. Dogs are pack animals and enjoy constant company. However, many dogs are alone in people's homes while the family works or goes to school. Birds cannot fly freely with other birds when they are confined to cages. Other pets that are burrowers, climbers, or swimmers have to carry out these natural behaviors in very cramped spaces. In addition, animal welfare organizations are concerned that pet owners do not always behave kindly toward their pets, or provide them with the best possible conditions.

There are laws in the United States and Canada that address animal cruelty and the abuse of pets. In 33 U.S. states and the District of Columbia, animal cruelty is treated as a **felony**. This means that it is a serious crime, and the person responsible for the abuse could go to prison for more than a year. The other states consider animal cruelty a **misdemeanor**. This means that it is not considered as serious a crime, and a prison term would last less than a year. In Canada, cruelty to animals is part of the country's **criminal code** and helps to protect pets from abuse and neglect.

Although we usually think of animals such as dogs and cats as pets, some people keep what are called **exotic pets**, including monkeys, snakes, and big cats such as tigers, cheetahs, or leopards. These kinds of animals have not been bred to be kept as pets. They are wild animals, and owners cannot look after them properly in their homes. They are also more likely than dogs and cats to injure their owners or carry diseases. In the United States, each state has different laws about keeping exotic animals as pets. In California, for example, no wild animals can be kept as pets. In contrast, in Oklahoma, you can own any kind of animal with a **permit**, which is a document that gives permission to do or have something. In Canada, the laws on ownership of exotic pets also differ between provinces, with some requiring permits and some banning the ownership of endangered animals.

So what are the arguments for and against animals being kept as pets?

29

Animals Should Be Kept as Pets.

Due to the benefits that both people and animals experience, animals should be kept as pets. Most pet owners love their animals and provide them with a safe home and a good life. Pets have warm homes, regular food, and treatment for illnesses and injuries. According to a 2015 poll, 95 percent of Americans say that their pet is a family member. Americans spent more than $66 billion on their pets in 2016. Canadians spent $4.1 billion on pets and pet food in 2015. Domesticated animals could not survive in the wild since they are used to living with humans. They also have longer life spans than wild animals. If it remains in good health, a pet dog can live until its mid-teens. The Australian wild dogs called dingoes live only 10 years in the wild.

Pets are good for people's health. Pets make people feel happy and less stressed, and can keep them fit and active through exercise. Animals can also help people who are unwell or recovering from illness. Studies at Purdue University found that elderly people suffering from **Alzheimer's disease** ate better and paid more attention to their surroundings if they had their meals in front of an aquarium containing bright-colored fish. Research in 2016 learned that children who struggled with reading aloud did better if they read to a trained dog and its handler. "Their attitudes change, and their skills improve," says Lisa Freeman, director of the Tufts Institute for Human-Animal Interaction. Even insects can be beneficial as pets. A 2016 study in *Gerontology* found that the moods of elderly people who were given crickets in a cage improved because they had something to take care of. Grooming horses or leading them on walks has been found to reduce the effects of **post-traumatic stress**

From an early age, children can learn to treat animals as companions. They also develop a sense of responsibility when looking after animals.

*Animals provide therapy in places such as hospitals, prisons, and nursing homes. Therapists who bring animals to sessions are often able to build a better **rapport** with patients.*

disorder (PTSD) in children and teenagers. Pet therapy is now seen as an important way to help patients of all ages recover from illness. "I don't know of any major children's hospital that doesn't have at least some kind of animal program," says Alan Beck, director of the Center for the Human-Animal Bond at Purdue University.

However, people argue that pet ownership is never beneficial if the animal is mistreated. Some owners feed their pets too much, others too little, and some owners do not provide animals with enough space, exercise, attention, or veterinary care. Yet the vast majority of owners are responsible people who love their pets very

much, look after them, and treat them as family members. Around 68 percent of U.S. owners give toys or other presents to their pets at Christmas, while 36 percent of Americans give their dogs birthday gifts. There are around 6,000 reported cases of dog abuse in the United States every year. However, this is a very small proportion when compared to the 70 million pet dogs in the country.

Based on the fact that keeping pets has been proven by scientific studies to be good for people's health and well-being, and that pet ownership is very beneficial for animals, pet ownership should continue.

Animals Should Not Be Kept as Pets.

Although pet ownership can sometimes be a good thing, the potential harm to animals that pet ownership causes is too great. Some pet owners do not look after their animals properly. Many do not have the time to give animals the care and exercise they need. Animals get neglected, dogs are not walked or trained, cat litter boxes are not emptied, and fish tanks or birdcages are not cleaned out. Sometimes animals are bought as presents for people who are not prepared to look after them. In the United Kingdom (UK), the Royal Society for the Prevention of Cruelty to Animals (RSPCA) says that three pets are abandoned every hour over the Christmas holidays because of being unwanted gifts. Some owners allow their pets to breed but then have no plans to find homes for the babies. Even when pet owners try to do their best for their pets, lack of knowledge may lead them to harm their pet. For example, many pet owners overfeed their dog so it becomes overweight, give their snake the wrong kind of food, or let their guinea pig's claws get too long.

"Pet owners, on average, spend far less than they should on veterinary care," says bioethicist Jessica Pierce, author of *Run, Spot, Run: The Ethics of Keeping Pets*. "At least a quarter of all dogs and cats never see a veterinarian, and millions live with untreated chronic pain or slow-moving illnesses that owners either fail to notice or are too tightfisted to address." Pierce also explains that pet animals are dependent on us, so when we leave for work, school, or vacations, it is very hard on their well-being. In 2015, Canadian shelters took in more than 82,000 cats and 35,000 dogs that had been abandoned or mistreated. In the United States, around 3.3 million dogs and 3.2 million cats enter shelters every year.

The pet industry is sometimes cruel to animals. There are laws governing the treatment of animals in the industry, but sometimes dogs, cats, rabbits, birds, fish, and other animals have poor living conditions and suffer injury or death.

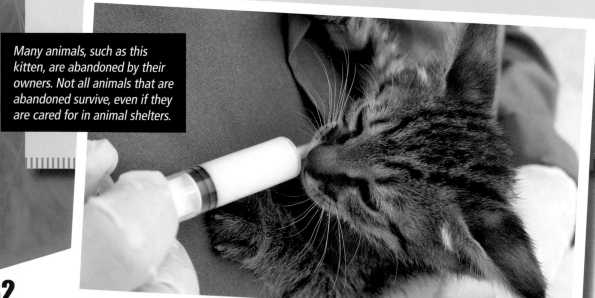

Many animals, such as this kitten, are abandoned by their owners. Not all animals that are abandoned survive, even if they are cared for in animal shelters.

Some dogs are born in **puppy mills** with poor living conditions and a lack of proper medical care. It is estimated that there are around 10,000 puppy mills in the United States, but fewer than 3,000 are regulated by the Department of Agriculture. "Puppy mills house breeding dogs in small, wire-floored cages, separate puppies from their mothers at a very young age, and ship them hundreds of miles to pet stores around the country," says Matt Bershadker, president and CEO of the ASPCA. In addition, some animals that are common as pets have been bred to make them look a certain way. This type of breeding has led to serious effects on animals' health. Pugs can have problems with their breathing, eyes, hips, and spine. Bulldogs have heart and skin issues. Labrador retrievers and German shepherds can have hip problems. Dogs that have very short legs can have severe back problems.

It is true that people do have the option to buy their pets from reputable breeders, animal shelters, and humane societies, where they are treated kindly. However, as a result of pets being abandoned or mistreated, 1.5 million shelter animals are euthanized in the United States every year. If people were not allowed to keep pets, these animals would not be killed.

Based on the fact that not all pet owners know how to look after animals or can neglect or mistreat them, combined with the terrible conditions that exist for some animals in the pet industry, animals should not be kept as pets.

Humans breed animals to meet their own preferences, but is this fair to the animals? Doesn't it cause some animals, such as pugs, discomfort and serious health problems?

33

STATE YOUR CASE

When it comes to any issue, you have to look at arguments on both sides before you decide where you stand. Remember the features of effective arguments when you think about arguments for and against whether animals should be kept as pets. Which argument do you think is the strongest? Give reasons for your answers. Use the "In Summary: For and Against" list to help you figure out your decision, and state your own case.

IN SUMMARY: FOR AND AGAINST

For Animals Being Kept as Pets

Most pet owners love their animals and provide them with a safe home and a good life.

- Pets have warm homes, regular food, and treatment for illnesses and injuries.
- Pets would not be able to survive in the wild since they are used to living with humans.
- Americans spent more than $66 billion on their pets in 2016.

Pets are good for people's health.

- Pets put their owners in a good mood, lower stress, and keep people fit and active.
- Animals can be used to help people to recover from illness.
- Elderly and lonely people who have pets often have better mental health.
- Research in 2016 learned that children who struggled with reading aloud did better if they read to a trained dog and its handler.
- Aquariums can help people who suffer from Alzheimer's disease.

Many pets are provided with very loving homes. Children grow up with their pets and spend a lot of time playing with them and caring for them.

Against Animals Being Kept as Pets

Some pet owners do not look after their animals properly.

- Some animals are bought as presents for people who are not prepared to care for them. Shelters often see higher numbers of unwanted animals after Christmas.
- Some animals are neglected by their owners and suffer as a result. Many owners spend less than they should on veterinary care.
- Some owners allow their pets to breed but have no plans for the babies, often resulting in them being abandoned.

The pet industry is sometimes cruel to animals.

- Some puppy mills give dogs poor living conditions and a lack of proper medical care.
- Of the 10,000 puppy mills in the United States, fewer than 3,000 are regulated by the Department of Agriculture.
- Some common pets, including pugs, bulldogs, Labrador retrievers, and German shepherds, have been bred to look a certain way, which has a bad effect on their health.

Pets are abandoned for different reasons. People move to smaller homes, the pet grows too large, or the owner dies and there is no one to look after the pet.

CHAPTER 5

SHOULD ANIMALS BE KEPT IN CAPTIVITY?

People can see animals such as lions, tigers, elephants, and gorillas in the wild, but most people cannot afford to travel to Africa or Asia where these animals live. For people in North America, zoos, aquariums, and safari parks are the only way that they will ever see these amazing creatures in person. However, not everyone is sure that keeping animals in captivity is a good thing.

Humans have kept animals in zoos for hundreds of years. Until the late twentieth century, many zoo animals lived in cramped concrete pens with metal bars. However, conditions have much improved in zoos in North America and Europe. Zoos now do their best to closely recreate the animal's natural environment. In safari parks, visitors can drive through the park and see animals roaming freely. The first safari park outside Africa opened in the UK in the 1960s. There are now safari parks in many countries. The first public aquarium for displaying water-living animals was opened in 1853 in London, UK.

The Work of Zoos, Aquariums, and Safari Parks

Some zoos work very hard to protect animals and save endangered species. For example, panda bears struggle to survive in the wild, where there are only around 1,800 animals. However, they are protected and live well in captivity, where the population is around 300. Other animals are killed by poachers in the wild, such as African elephants and rhinos. In South Africa, 68 elephants and 1,028 rhinos were killed by poachers in 2017. So many are killed that the species could be driven to extinction. While work continues to stop poaching, zoos make sure that at least some of these animals are protected. In addition, zoos and safari parks play a role in educating people about animals, their habitats, and the threats they face.

Zoos, aquariums, and wildlife parks also make money from visitors. In North America, money made by these facilities is put back into providing captive animals with the best possible living conditions. Sometimes, money also goes toward conservation programs in the animals' natural habitats. For example, many North American zoos and aquariums are part of the Species Survival

Pandas are from China, but many people have been able to view the animals in zoos. Pandas have been endangered for many years, but are now protected.

Plan (SSP) Program run by the Association of Zoos and Aquariums (AZA). The organization raises awareness and money for habitat protection and field projects for specific species.

Questions About Captivity

Many people believe that animals should be left in the wild and not kept in captivity in zoos, aquariums, and safari parks. Even though animals are usually well treated in zoos and parks, people opposed to them do not think that we have the right to keep animals on display just to amuse or educate humans. Few zoos, aquariums, or wildlife parks have enough space to provide larger animals with the space they would have to roam in the wild. Lions and tigers have around 18,000 times less space in captivity than they would have in their natural habitat. Polar bears have 1 million times less space than they would have in the Arctic. Roadside zoos, petting zoos, and smaller operations usually have even less space for the animals.

Zoos, safari parks, and aquariums are very popular places to visit. They are often the only opportunity people have to see animals from all over the world.

So what are the arguments for and against keeping animals in captivity in zoos, aquariums, and safari parks?

ZOOS BY NUMBERS

Here are some interesting statistics about zoos and safari parks:

- There are more than 10,000 zoos worldwide.
- These zoos are home to around 1 million vertebrates, or animals with a backbone.
- Every year, around 600 million people visit zoos.
- Zoo Berlin in Germany has the world's largest collection of animals, with more than 15,000 animals from 1,700 species.
- The U.S. Association of Zoos and Aquariums includes 215 zoos that spend $160 million on conservation every year.

Keeping Animals in Captivity Should Be Allowed.

Zoos, aquariums, and safari parks help to protect endangered species. Zoos save endangered species by moving them to a safe setting, where they are safe from hunters, poachers, and predators, and protected from the loss of their habitat in the wild. Some zoos have breeding programs that also help to increase the population of endangered species. In North America, zoos that are part of the AZA's Species Survival Plan (SSP) manage the breeding of endangered species to make sure there are enough of the animals to save them from extinction. AZA runs 113 different SSPs for 181 individual species. The programs have helped many animals avoid extinction in the last few decades. The Arabian oryx was hunted to extinction in the wild, but there are now more than 1,000 in the wild and many more in captivity because of zoo conservation programs led by The Phoenix Zoo in Arizona. There were once only 27 California condors, a huge bird, left alive—

but the San Diego Wild Animal Park and the Los Angeles Zoo helped them survive. There are now hundreds of the birds living in the state. In Asia, hunters and loss of habitat drove the Amur leopard close to extinction. Today, there are more than 200 of the animals in zoos around the world. Zoos are also studying different animal diseases to help protect both zoo and wild animals from them. For example, there are 20 experts at the San Diego Zoo who study wildlife diseases.

Zoos, aquariums, and safari parks help people learn more about animals and appreciate them. This supports wildlife conservation because more people learn about the importance of protecting animals. Zoos and aquariums approved by the AZA educate more than 180 million visitors every year, including 51 million students. Education programs focus on wild animals, their habitats, how they might be in danger, and the ways that humans can help them survive. In the last

Most safari parks have large African animals, such as the elephant, giraffe, lion, rhinoceros, and hippopotamus. These animals usually roam free in the parks.

10 years, AZA-approved schools and colleges have also trained more than 400,000 teachers about animals and conservation. In 2014, 146,136 students took part in educational programs with Zoos Victoria in Australia. "Zoos and aquariums are in a unique position to contribute to the goal of raising understanding of **biodiversity** conservation," says Eric Jensen from the UK's University of Warwick's sociology department.

People who are opposed to zoos claim that some zoo animals live in poor conditions and are mistreated. In 2016, for example, staff at Papanack Zoo, a roadside zoo near Ottawa, Canada, admitted to beating a lion cub to "train" it. It is true that there are some loopholes in the law that allow some smaller zoos to escape regulation, but most zoos are well run and are dedicated to animal welfare. In the United States, the best zoos need to meet strict standards for animal care set by the AZA. Canada's Accredited Zoos and Aquariums (CAZA) does similar work. Other countries also have organizations to protect animals, such as the British and Irish Association of Zoos and Aquariums (BIAZA) and the European Association of Zoos and Aquaria (EAZA).

Based on the fact that zoos, aquariums, and safari parks work hard to protect endangered species, are regulated by zoo associations, provide animals with a safe environment, and educate people about animals and conservation, they should not be banned. Both animals and people would be worse off if zoos, aquariums, and safari parks did not exist.

The Arabian oryx became extinct in the wild in 1972 before being saved. In 2011, the total wild population was more than 1,000.

Animals Should Not Be Kept in Captivity.

Due to the harm that zoos, aquariums, and safari parks cause to animals, they should be banned. Animals are sometimes mistreated in zoos, aquariums, and safari parks. They can have very poor living conditions and are kept confined for much of the time. Animals should not be taken from their natural environment. Polar bears do not belong in the hot Florida sun, lions do not belong in Canada, and killer whales do not belong in small pools. Although most zoos and safari parks in North America and Western Europe provide good care, there have been issues with facilities around the world. Between 2013 and 2016 at South Lakes Safari Zoo in Cumbria, in the UK, almost 500 animals died, some from such things as lack of food, **hypothermia**, and collisions with cars. At the Hangzhou Safari Park in China in 2017, staff were filmed whipping white tigers to make them perform for the public. In North America, Wildlife Safari in Winston, Oregon, was found to have forced elephants to give car washes for visitors to the park. In some petting zoos, animals are on display for long periods and do not receive proper care. In 2018, the owner of a petting zoo in British Columbia was charged with 24 counts of animal cruelty. "Most petting zoos use baby animals who are not used to being handled," says Australian RSPCA Metropolitan Inspector Natalie Will. "They're being transported around and then left in an intense situation with up to 30 children who might not know how to be gentle with animals."

Zoos, aquariums, and safari parks sometimes cause health problems for captive animals. When animals are removed from their natural environment, they sometimes develop physical or mental health issues. Most of these are problems

Some animals suffer from great stress when forced to interact with tourists or pose for photographs. People and animals have sometimes been hurt in these situations.

Animals have sometimes been injured by visitors at zoos. They may be given food that they don't usually eat and get sick as a result.

that only come from captivity, which the animals do not experience in the wild. Even if zoos try hard to recreate the animal's natural environment, it is often far from the natural habitats animals need to live healthy lives. Animals that are bored or lonely can sometimes develop mental problems. **Zoochosis** is a condition that causes captive animals to rock, sway, or pace, which means that they walk back and forth repeatedly. Some affected animals hurt themselves by chewing parts of their body or pulling out their fur or feathers. According to 2003 research published in *Nature* magazine, lions in captivity spend 48 percent of their time pacing. Some zoos give animals medication to stop this behavior. Gus the polar bear lived at the Central Park Zoo in New York. He would swim obsessively for up to 12 hours every day, but this behavior slowed down once he was given **Prozac**. This is a drug that is given to people suffering from **depression** and could cause harm in animals. A 2013 study of 225 captive elephants in zoos in the UK found that 75 percent were overweight. Elephants also develop foot problems in captivity as a result of

being kept in enclosures with hard surfaces. A study found that of a sample of elephants living in enclosures with hard surfaces in the UK, 80.4 percent had foot problems.

It is true that most zoos are regulated to ensure that animals are treated well. The AZA regulates zoos in the United States, and Canada's Accredited Zoos and Aquariums (CAZA) regulates zoos in Canada. However, this is not the case with all zoos. There are roadside, traveling zoos across the United States, and most of them are not licensed by AZA. Roadside zoos also do not need to have qualified staff to look after the animals. There is no way to make sure that all animals kept in captivity are safe and well cared for.

Although it may be great to see animals from around the world, captivity is wrong. The harm that is caused to animals by taking them from their natural environment, and the mistreatment that many zoo and safari park animals experience, is enough to prove that zoos, aquariums, and safari parks should be banned.

STATE YOUR CASE

When it comes to any issue, you have to look at arguments on both sides before you decide where you stand. Remember the features of effective arguments when you think about arguments for and against keeping animals in captivity in zoos, aquariums, and safari parks. Which argument do you think is the most convincing? Why? Use the "In Summary: For and Against" list to help you figure out your decision, and state your own case.

IN SUMMARY: FOR AND AGAINST

Against Keeping Animals in Captivity

Animals are sometimes mistreated in zoos, aquariums, and safari parks.

- Animals should not be taken from their natural environment. Enclosures in captivity cannot compare to their natural habitat. Sometimes animals have very poor living conditions and are kept confined for much of the time.
- At South Lakes Safari Zoo in Cumbria, in the UK, almost 500 animals died between 2013 and 2016, from such things as lack of food, hypothermia, and collisions with cars.
- Wildlife Safari in Winston, Oregon, forced elephants to give car washes for visitors.
- In some petting zoos, animals are on display for long periods and do not receive proper care.

Zoos, aquariums, and safari parks sometimes cause health problems for captive animals.

- Zoochosis is a condition that causes captive animals to rock, sway, or pace much of the time. Lions spend 48 percent of their time pacing when in captivity.
- Some zoos give animals medication to stop obsessive behavior. This could harm them.
- A 2013 study of 225 elephants in captivity in UK zoos found that 75 percent were overweight, and many had foot problems as a result of hard surfaces.

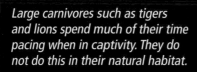

Large carnivores such as tigers and lions spend much of their time pacing when in captivity. They do not do this in their natural habitat.

For Allowing Animals to Be Kept in Captivity

Zoos, aquariums, and safari parks help protect endangered species.

- Zoos save endangered species by moving them to a safe setting away from hunters, poachers, predators, and habitat loss.
- Some zoos have breeding programs to build back the populations of species that are endangered. Zoos have saved many species from extinction.
- In North America, many zoos are part of the AZA's Species Survival Plan.

Zoos, aquariums, and safari parks help people learn more about animals and can raise support for conservation efforts.

- Zoos provide education about animals and why they need protection.
- Zoos and aquariums approved by the AZA educate around 180 million visitors a year.
- AZA-approved schools and colleges have trained more than 400,000 teachers about animals and conservation.
- 146,136 students took part in educational programs with Zoos Victoria in Australia in 2014.

Zoos allow children to see animals that they have few opportunities to see in their natural environment. The children also learn about the animals and how they can play a role in protecting them.

BIBLIOGRAPHY

Animals Today and Tomorrow

Barkham, Patrick. "Nearly 20,000 Badgers Culled in Attempt to Reduce Bovine TB." *The Guardian*, December 21, 2017. www.theguardian.com/environment/2017/dec/21/nearly-20000-badgers-culled-in-attempt-to-reduce-bovine-tb

Briggs, Helen. "Q&A: The Badger Cull." *BBC News*, August 27, 2013. www.bbc.com/news/science-environment-22614350

Bullen, Vivien. "How Selective Culling Works." How Stuff Works. https://adventure.howstuffworks.com/outdoor-activities/hunting/game-handling/selective-culling2.htm

Bulman, May. "Australia to Cull More Than a Million Kangaroos This Year." *The Independent*, February 16, 2017. www.independent.co.uk/news/world/australasia/australia-kangaroos-culling-killing-murder-deaths-a-year-a7583186.html

"Culling Animals." *BBC News*. http://news.bbc.co.uk/cbbcnews/hi/find_out/guides/animals/culling_animals/newsid_3552000/3552512.stm

"Culling Pest Animals Can Do More Harm Than Good." The Conversation, March 7, 2015. http://theconversation.com/culling-pest-animals-can-do-more-harm-than-good-40702

Doward, Jamie. "Badger Cull Faces Review as Bovine TB Goes on Rising." *The Guardian*, March 4, 2018. www.theguardian.com/environment/2018/mar/04/badger-cull-government-review-bovine-tb-inquiry

Fears, Darryl. "The Dirty Dozen: 12 of the Most Destructive Invasive Animals in the United States." *The Washington Post*, February 23, 2015. https://www.washingtonpost.com/news/energy-environment/wp/2015/02/23/like-most-invasive-species-pythons-are-in-the-u-s-to-stay/?noredirect=on&utm_term=.df02948df428

James, Will. "Killing Wildlife: The Pros and Cons of Culling Animals." *National Geographic*, March 6, 2014. https://news.nationalgeographic.com/news/2014/03/140305-culling-badgers-deer-bison-swans-ethics-conservation

"Questions & Answers about Bison Management." National Park Service. www.nps.gov/yell/learn/management/bison-management-faqs.htm

"Staying Safe in Crocodile Country: Culling Isn't The Answer." The Conversation, June 1, 2016. http://theconversation.com/staying-safe-in-crocodile-country-culling-isnt-the-answer-60252

"Why Kangaroo Culling Divides Australia." *BBC News*, February 15, 2017. http://www.bbc.com/news/world-australia-38964535

What Makes an Argument?

"8 Big Pros and Cons of Wolf Reintroduction." Connect US. https://connectusfund.org/8-big-pros-and-cons-of-wolf-reintroduction

Brenner, Laurie. "The Pros and Cons of Cloning." Sciencing, July 20, 2018. https://sciencing.com/pros-cons-cloning-5453902.html

"Cloning Dolly the Sheep." Animal Research Info. www.animalresearch.info/en/medical-advances/timeline/cloning-dolly-the-sheep

Conners, Bill. "Why Hunting Is a Good Thing, No Matter the Public Opinion." *Poughkeepsie Journal*, December 9, 2015. www.poughkeepsiejournal.com/story/sports/recreational/2015/12/09/hunting-good-thing-matter-public-opinion/77044276

Erickson, Jim. "Vampire Bats Spread Rabies in Latin America. Does Culling Help?" University of Michigan, December 2, 2013. https://global.umich.edu/newsroom/vampire-bats-spread-rabies-in-latin-america-does-culling-help

Giese, Jeanna. "Experience: I Was Bitten by a Rabid Bat." *The Guardian*, August 26, 2016. www.theguardian.com/lifeandstyle/2016/aug/26/experience-bitten-by-rabid-bat

Girard, Patrick. "What Are Arguments?" Future Learn, University of Auckland. www.futurelearn.com/courses/logical-and-critical-thinking/0/steps/9137

Gonchar, Michael. "200 Prompts for Argumentative Writing." *The New York Times*, February 4, 2014. https://learning.blogs.nytimes.com/2014/02/04/200-prompts-for-argumentative-writing

"Gray Wolves Increase Tourism in Yellowstone National Park." Yellowstone Park, June 21, 2011. www.yellowstonepark.com/things-to-do/gray-wolves-increase-tourism-in-yellowstone-national-park

Lombardo, Crystal. "Pros and Cons of Hunting." Vision Launch, February 9, 2016. http://visionlaunch.com/pros-and-cons-of-hunting

Lombardo, Crystal. "Pros and Cons of Wolf Reintroduction." Vision Launch, April 12, 2016. http://visionlaunch.com/pros-and-cons-of-wolf-reintroduction

Peglar, Tori. "1995 Reintroduction of Wolves in Yellowstone." Yellowstone Park, July 9, 2018. www.yellowstonepark.com/park/yellowstone-wolves-reintroduction

Robertson, Josh. "Trophy Hunting." Conservation Conversation, October 18, 2016. www.conservationconversation.co.uk/trophy-hunting

Schulten, Katherine. "10 Ways to Teach Argument-Writing with *The New York Times*." *The New York Times*, October 5, 2017. www.nytimes.com/2017/10/05/learning/lesson-plans/10-ways-to-teach-argument-writing-with-the-new-york-times.html

Shultz, David. "Should We Bring Extinct Species Back From the Dead?" *Science Magazine*, September 26, 2016. www.sciencemag.org/news/2016/09/should-we-bring-extinct-species-back-dead

Strauss, Bob. "Can We Clone a Woolly Mammoth?" Thoughtco, November 17, 2017. www.thoughtco.com/can-we-clone-a-woolly-mammoth-1091997

"What Is Argument?" AEGEE Europe, June 5, 2014. www.zeus.aegee.org/debate/what-is-argument

"Why Sport Hunting Is Cruel and Unnecessary." PETA. www.peta.org/issues/wildlife/wildlife-factsheets/sport-hunting-cruel-unnecessary

Should Animals Be Used in Rodeo Sports?

Esrock, Robin. "7 Myths About Animal Treatment at the Calgary Stampede Rodeo." Matador Network, June 28, 2012. https://matadornetwork.com/change/7-myths-about-animal-treatment-at-the-calgary-stampede-rodeo

"Humane Facts." Friends of Rodeo. www.friendsofrodeoinc.com/humane-facts

Kienlen, Alexis. "Stampede Is a Champion of Animal Welfare, Says Researcher." *Alberta Farm Express*, April 11, 2017. www.albertafarmexpress.ca/2017/04/11/stampede-is-a-champion-of-animal-welfare-says-researcher

Larson, Peggy. "Rodeos: Inherent Cruelty to Animals." Humane Society Veterinary Medical Association, January 15, 2015. www.hsvma.org/rodeos_inherent_cruelty_to_animals

"Rodeo." Encyclopedia Britannica. www.britannica.com/sports/rodeo-sport

"Rodeos." PETA. www.peta.org/issues/animals-in-entertainment/cruel-sports/rodeos

"Rodeos." Vancouver Humane Society. www.vancouverhumanesociety.bc.ca/campaigns/rodeos

Rowe, Claudia. "Pros and Cons of Rodeo Roping and Riding." *The New York Times*, June 16, 2002. www.nytimes.com/2002/06/16/nyregion/pros-and-cons-of-rodeo-roping-and-riding.html

Ryan, Jennifer. "Rodeos Put Animal Care Front & Center." *Beef Magazine*, March 5, 2013. www.beefmagazine.com/cattle-handling/rodeos-put-animal-care-front-center

Should Animals Be Kept as Pets?

"Animal Cruelty Laws." Ontario SPCA. http://ontariospca.ca/what-we-do/investigations/animal-cruelty-laws.html

"Canadian Animal Shelter Statistics." Humane Canada. www.humanecanada.ca/animal_shelter_statistics_report

Crawford, Amy. "Is It Ethical to Keep Pets?" *The Boston Globe*, May 15, 2016. www.bostonglobe.com/ideas/2016/05/14/ethical-keep-pets/nB3VciaZzJKWUqOlmJVZ2J/story.html

"Facts about Pet Ownership in Canada." Pet Backer. www.petbacker.com/blog/facts/facts-about-pet-ownership-in-canada

"Fish Aquarium Tanks and Alzheimer's Dementia." Alzheimer's Support. www.free-alzheimers-support.com/home-aquarium-tanks-and-alzheimers-dementia

Grimm, David. "A Dog That Lives 300 Years? Solving the Mysteries of Aging in our Pets." *Science Magazine*, December 3, 2015. www.sciencemag.org/news/2015/12/feature-dog-lives-300-years-solving-mysteries-aging-our-pets

Newport, Frank, et al. "Americans and Their Pets." Gallup, December 21, 2006. http://news.gallup.com/poll/25969/americans-their-pets.aspx

Oaklander, Mandy. "Science Says Your Pet Is Good for Your Mental Health." *Time*, April 6, 2017. http://time.com/4728315/science-says-pet-good-for-mental-health

Paddon, Natalie. "Canadians Spend Billions on Spoiled Pets." *Hamilton Spectator*, August 10, 2016. www.thespec.com/news-story/6802056-hamilton-business-canadians-spend-billions-on-spoiled-pets

Rodriguez McRobbie, Linda. "Should We Stop Keeping Pets?" *The Guardian*, August 1, 2017. www.theguardian.com/lifeandstyle/2017/aug/01/should-we-stop-keeping-pets-why-more-and-more-ethicists-say-yes

"Shelter Intake and Surrender." ASPCA. https://www.aspca.org/animal-homelessness/shelter-intake-and-surrender/pet-statistics

Stevens, Sidney. "Pets Are Good for Your Health, and We Have the Studies to Prove It." Mother Nature Network, April 6, 2018. www.mnn.com/family/pets/stories/11-studies-that-prove-pets-are-good-your-health

Tucker, Jo. "A Pet's Life Expectancy: How Long Will My Pet Live?" Pet Helpful, October 17, 2017. https://pethelpful.com/misc/Pet-Life-Expectancy-The-Lifespans-of-Popular-Pets

"U.S. Pet Ownership Statistics." American Veterinary Medical Association. www.avma.org/KB/Resources/Statistics/Pages/Market-research-statistics-US-pet-ownership.aspx

Should Animals Be Kept in Captivity?

"10 Endangered Species Saved from Extinction By Zoos." Taronga Conservation Society Australia. https://taronga.org.au/news/2017-05-22/10-endangered-species-saved-extinction-zoos

Benjamin, Alison, and Toby Moses. "Should Zoos Be Banned?" *The Guardian*, June 1, 2016. www.theguardian.com/commentisfree/2016/jun/01/should-zoos-be-banned-head-to-head

"Can Zoos Save the World?" The Conversation, October 30, 2014. https://theconversation.com/can-zoos-save-the-world-32356

"Conservation Education." Association of Zoos and Aquariums. www.aza.org/conservation-education

Dell 'Amore, Christine. "Is Breeding Pandas in Captivity Worth It?" *National Geographic*, August 28, 2013. https://news.nationalgeographic.com/news/2013/08/130827-giant-panda-national-zoo-baby-breeding-animals-science

"Elephant Poaching Statistics." Poaching Facts. www.poachingfacts.com/poaching-statistics/elephant-poaching-statistics

"Five Facts About Good Zoos." Zoos Victoria, October 1, 2015. www.zoo.org.au/news/five-facts-about-good-zoos#FACT2

Ganzert, Dr. Robin. "Zoos Are Not Prisons. They Improve the Lives of Animals." *Time*, June 13, 2016. http://time.com/4364671/zoos-improve-lives-of-animals

Gulledge, Jacqueline. "Zoo Atlanta's Mission to Help Save Pandas." *CNN*, March 29, 2016. www.cnn.com/2016/03/29/us/iyw-panda-conservation-zoo-atlanta/index.html

Hoare, Philip. "All Zoos Should Be Closed: Other Species Have Rights." *The Guardian*, October 2, 2017. https://www.theguardian.com/commentisfree/2017/oct/02/zoos-closed-nearly-500-animals-die-four-years-zoo

Horton, Jennifer. "Are Zoos Good or Bad for Animals?" How Stuff Works. https://animals.howstuffworks.com/animal-facts/zoos-good-or-bad.htm

"How Do Zoos Help Endangered Animals?" *Scientific American*, www.scientificamerican.com/article/how-do-zoos-help-endangered-animals

"How Wildlife Tourism and Zoos Can Protect Animals in the Wild." The Conversation, May 18, 2014. http://theconversation.com/how-wildlife-tourism-and-zoos-can-protect-animals-in-the-wild-26521

Lin, Doris. "Arguments For and Against Zoos." Thoughtco, May 9, 2018. www.thoughtco.com/arguments-for-and-against-zoos-127639

Neff, Michelle. "Are Safaris Okay for Animals Lovers? How to Tell the Difference if an Attraction Is Harmful to Animals." One Green Planet, January 12, 2108. www.onegreenplanet.org/animalsandnature/are-safaris-ever-okay-for-animal-lovers

Page, Lee. "What 5,000 People Learned at the Zoo." Futurity, March 18, 2015. www.futurity.org/zoos-education-biodiversity-878672

Panagiotopolou, Olga. "Why Elephants in Captivity Sometimes Suffer from Sore Feet." University of Queensland, January 2, 2017. https://medicine.uq.edu.au/article/2017/01/why-elephants-kept-captivity-suffer-sore-feet

"Poaching Statistics." Save the Rhino. www.savetherhino.org/rhino_info/poaching_statistics

Thoet, Alison. "How Are U.S. Zoos Keeping Animals Safe?" *PBS*, March 22, 2017. www.pbs.org/newshour/science/u-s-zoos-keeping-animals-safe

GLOSSARY

Please note: Some **boldfaced** words are defined where they appear in the text.

adapted Changed to suit a different set of conditions

Alzheimer's disease A disease causing the brain to deteriorate

animal welfare The protection of the health or well-being of animals

biodiversity The variety of plant and animal life

bred Kept for the purpose of producing young animals with desirable characteristics

bronc riding A rodeo event in which a person rides a kicking or bucking horse

bullfighting An event in which humans try to kill bulls

campaigning Working toward achieving a goal

captivity Being kept somewhere and not allowed to leave

chuck wagon A covered horse-drawn wagon

chute The narrow entrance to a rodeo ring

cloning Artificially producing an animal or plant from the cells of another animal or plant

conservation Protecting plants and animals

cosmetics Products applied to the body to improve its appearance

credible Believable or convincing

criminal code A document that includes all of a country's laws against crime

culling The process of reducing wild animal numbers in a particular area

depression Feelings of great sadness over a long period of time

docile Easy to control

domesticated Tamed or brought under control

economy The prosperity and earnings of a place, such as a country, city, or town

ecosystem A biological community of organisms and their natural environment

ethical Relating to beliefs about what is right and wrong

euthanized Killed to relieve suffering from an incurable illness or injury

evidence Anything, such as data or statistics, that proves or disproves something

exotic pets Rare or unusual pets that are usually considered wild animals

extinction When no members of a species exist

factory farms Farms where poultry, pigs, or cattle are kept indoors under very controlled conditions

gender The state of being male or female

GPS An acronym for Global Positioning System; a navigation system that uses satellites and computers to determine a location on Earth's surface

great auk A large extinct bird that lived around the North Atlantic Ocean

habitats The natural environments of living things

hypothermia A condition in which the body temperature has become dangerously low as a result of being in severe cold for a long time

industries Businesses that make goods or provide services

invasive species A species that is not native to an ecosystem

life expectancy How long someone or something is expected to live

logic A system of thinking and figuring out ideas

mental health A person or animal's mental and emotional well-being

natural resources Materials, such as minerals, forests, water, and fertile land, that are used by people

overfishing Fishing excessively so that species are reduced

overgrazing When plants are eaten by animals for extended periods of time

overpopulation More animals living in an area than can be supported by the environment there

packs Groups of wild animals that live and hunt together

persuade To convince somebody to agree with you

poaching Hunting animals illegally and selling the animals' horns, tusks, or other body parts for profit

post-traumatic stress disorder (PTSD) A condition of mental and emotional stress caused by injury or severe shock

predators Animals that hunt and eat other animals

prey An animal that is hunted by other animals for food

prod A handheld electrical device designed to give cattle a small shock

puppy mills Places that breed puppies for sale, often in poor conditions

quagga An extinct subspecies of zebra

rabies A contagious and fatal disease in dogs and other mammals

rapport A good relationship

rodeo sports Public events in which professionals show different skills, including catching cattle with ropes

rural From or in the countryside

safari parks Large enclosed areas where wild animals live freely. People can pay to drive through the parks.

service animals Animals trained to assist people with disabilities

species A group of plants or animals that are alike in many ways

spurs Spiked devices worn on a rider's heels, used to urge an animal forward

statistics Facts involving numbers or data

steer A young male ox

Steller's sea cow An extinct marine mammal similar to a manatee

tissue The materials, such as muscle and fat, from which animals and plants are made

trophy hunting The hunting of wild animals for sport. The trophy is the animal or part of animal kept and displayed.

valid Something that is sound or well founded

vulnerable In need of protection to avoid extinction

LEARNING MORE

Find out more about the arguments concerning animals.

Books

Castaldo, Nancy. *Back from the Brink: Saving Animals from Extinction.*
HMH Books for Young Readers, 2018.

Laidlaw, Rob. *On Parade: The Hidden World of Animals in Entertainment.* Fitzhenry & Whiteside, 2010.

Terp, Gail. *The Debate About Animal Testing* (Pros and Cons). Focus Readers, 2018.

Zoehfeld, Kathleen Weidner. *Wild Lives: A History of People & Animals of the Bronx Zoo.*
Knopf Books for Young Readers, 2006.

Websites

Find out about the history of rodeo and rodeo events at:
www.britannica.com/sports/rodeo-sport

Learn more about writing and evaluating arguments and counterclaims:
www.icivics.org/products/drafting-board

For more information on the pros and cons of culling animals, visit:
https://news.nationalgeographic.com/news/2014/03/140305-culling-badgers-deer-bison-swans-ethics-conservation

Read more about the issues surrounding keeping animals in zoos at:
https://ww2.kqed.org/education/2016/05/11/should-animals-be-kept-in-zoos

INDEX

ABOUT THE AUTHOR

Simon Rose is an author of 15 novels and more than 100 nonfiction books. He offers programs for schools, covering the writing process, editing and revision, where ideas come from, character development, historical fiction, story structure, and the publishing world. He is an instructor for adults and offers online workshops and courses. Simon also provides services for writers, including manuscript evaluation, editing, and coaching, plus copywriting services for the business community.